This Little Tiger book belongs to:

_____

_____

_____

For my Mum
Hanako Clulow

LiTTLE TiGER
LONDON

LITTLE TIGER
An imprint of Little Tiger Press Limited
www.littletiger.co.uk
1 Coda Studios, 189 Munster Road, London SW6 6AW
Imported into the EEA by Penguin Random House Ireland,
Morrison Chambers, 32 Nassau Street, Dublin D02 YH68
First published in Great Britain 2020
This edition published in 2022
Text by Jonny Marx • Text copyright © Caterpillar Books Ltd 2020
Illustrations copyright © Hanako Clulow 2020
All rights reserved • Printed in China
A CIP catalogue record of this book is available from the British Library
ISBN: 978-1-83891-418-9 • CPB/2700/2419/0323
2 4 6 8 10 9 7 5 3

The Journey

Nature's Greatest Adventure

The Migration

Every year, thousands of zebras sense a change in weather patterns and begin roving towards more fertile grasslands in order to find food. This happens across the African continent as different herds roam the landscape.

One herd in Namibia makes the longest migration of any African land mammal, spanning 240km (150mi) in just two weeks. The zebras chomp at the lush grass for two months before making the long trek back again!

The most famous zebra migrations take place in the Maasai Mara and Serengeti National Parks, where many other creatures converge. Huge crocodiles that live in the rivers in these regions also hope to fill their bellies, but zebras are strong swimmers and many escape to continue nature's greatest adventure.

Written by Jonny Marx

Illustrated by Hanako Clulow

On arid plains, in soaring heat,
Starts one of nature's greatest feats.

Across the landscape, zebras stride,
As though they sense a turning tide.

Some creatures must now leave the glade,
While lions slumber in the shade.

Wild animals stomp and flap and run
Beneath the Serengeti sun.

Birds flock from all across the sky
Towards tall trees that soar up high.

Some hitch rides on elephants' backs,
Through weaving, winding, dusty tracks.

The tallest creatures in the land
Walk through dirt, through wind, through sand.

They chew at leaves until they're gone,
While zebras journey on and on.

Animals line up side by side,
At last it's time to break their stride.

Parched creatures rush to quench and swill,
All drinking till they've had their fill.

The beasts all stop, ears pricked, alert,
As something skulks beneath the dirt.

They rush and swim, they cannot rest,
For this is nature's greatest test.

When they reach the pastures green
And grass is all that can be seen...

The animals can bask in rain...

Before the long trek home again.

Plains zebra

The plains zebra lives in regions of eastern and southern Africa. It is the most common of the zebra species, but by no means ordinary!

Each zebra's stripes are completely unique in pattern.

The zebra's iconic stripes are thought to confuse predators, such as lions, hyenas and cheetahs, and deter mosquitos and flying pests, acting like a natural bug repellent.

A zebra has a fierce kick, strong enough to kill a lion.

Zebras are fast – they can run at speeds of up to 61 kmph – that's 17 m per second.

Blue wildebeest

Common agama

Cape buffalo

Nile crocodile

Black rhinoceros

Common warthog

Gemsbok

Common ostrich

Great egret

African crowned crane

African leopard

Fischer's lovebird

Greater blue-eared starling

Mangrove kingfisher

Lion

Maasai giraffe

African spurred tortoise

African elephant

Springbok